The Life of George Washington

Jed Abbey

INFOMAX COMMON CORE READERS

Rosen Classroom™

New York

Published in 2013 by The Rosen Publishing Group, Inc.
29 East 21st Street, New York, NY 10010

Book Design: Katelyn Londino

Photo Credits: Cover, p. 19 Buyenlarge/Contributor/Archive Photos/Getty Images; pp. 4, 10 Hulton Archive/Stringer/Hulton Archive/Getty Images; pp. 5, 8, 14 PhotoQuest/Contributor/Archive Photos/Getty Images; pp. 6, 12, 15 UniversalImagesGroup/Contributor/Universal Images Group/Getty Images; pp. 7, 23 (Mount Vernon) American School/The Bridgeman Art Library/Getty Images; pp. 9, 20 Stock Montage/Contributor/Archive Photos/Getty Images; p. 11 Popperfoto/Contributor/Popperfoto/Getty Images; pp. 13, 23 (Valley Forge) SuperStock/SuperStock/Getty Images; p. 16 Three Lions/Stringer/Hulton Archive/Getty Images; p. 17 Hulton Archive/Staff/Hulton Archive/Getty Images; p. 18 MPI/Stringer/Archive Photos/Getty Images; p. 21 Robert Pernell/Shutterstock.com.

ISBN: 978-1-4488-8986-0
6-pack ISBN: 978-1-4488-8987-7

Manufactured in the United States of America

CPSIA Compliance Information: Batch #WS12RC: For further information contact Rosen Publishing, New York, New York at 1-800-237-9932.

Word Count: 193

Contents

George Washington was
our first president.

George was born on February 22, 1732.

George's life wasn't easy.

His father died when he was 11 years old.

In 1752, George became the owner of a big farm.
The farm's name is Mount Vernon.

England ruled America at that time. In 1754, George helped England fight a war with France.

In 1759, George got married.

His wife's name was Martha.

George wasn't happy with England.
He didn't want to pay taxes to England.

People in America wanted to be free.
They went to war with England in 1775.

George led the army during the war.

In 1777, George's army came to a place called Valley Forge.

They stayed there for the winter.

The army was cold and hungry.

George helped the army during the hard winter. He was a good leader.

George helped America win the war!

The war ended in 1781.

People chose George
to become America's first president.

George started his job as president in 1789.

Americans chose George
to be president again in 1793.

George died on December 14, 1799.

Americans were sad when he died.

We still honor George Washington today!

George Washington's Life

1732 George is born.

1775 America's war against England starts.

1781 America wins the war against England.

1789 George becomes the first president of the United States.

1799 George dies.

Words to Know

Mount Vernon

Valley Forge

Index